NATIONAL
GEOGRAPH

Lighter on the Moon

Jeanne and Bradley Weaver

Contents

To the Moon

Astronauts Neil Armstrong and Edwin "Buzz" Aldrin were the first people to walk on the moon. On July 20, 1969, their spacecraft landed on the moon's surface. Their **mission** helped us to learn about the moon.

Astronaut Edwin "Buzz" Aldrin steps off the spacecraft to begin his walk on the moon.

The astronauts explored the surface of the moon. They collected rocks and soil. They learned how it felt to stand, walk, and jump on the moon. They also learned what it was like to be lighter on the moon.

Did you know that things weigh less on the moon than they do on Earth? It's true. Astronauts weigh less when they are on the moon than when they are on Earth. And it's all because of **gravity**!

Astronaut Buzz Aldrin prepares to do tests on the moon.

The astronauts wore heavy space suits on the moon.

What Is Gravity?

Have you ever noticed that no matter how high you throw a ball, it always comes back to the ground? This happens because of gravity. Gravity is a force that pulls. Earth has gravity. It pulls on you and other objects. Without gravity, a thrown ball would keep going up and out into space.

Gravity helps us juggle and play other ball games.

Gravity and Weight

Gravity keeps us on the ground. It also determines our **weight.** How can that be? Think about how much you weigh. Your weight is determined by how much Earth's gravity pulls on you. If Earth had less gravity, you would weigh less.

No matter how high you jump, Earth's gravity pulls you back to the ground.

Gravity on the Moon

Like Earth, all objects have gravity. The amount of gravity an object has depends on its size. Compare the size of the moon to the size of Earth. The moon is much smaller than Earth.

The moon does not have as much gravity as Earth. Gravity on Earth is six times greater than it is on the moon. Because the moon has less gravity, objects weigh less on the moon than they do on Earth.

Moon

Earth is much bigger
than the moon.

Earth

Feeling Gravity

When Neil Armstrong and Buzz Aldrin stepped out of their spacecraft, they found out what it felt like to be lighter on the moon. Even with their heavy space suits on, they could jump farther on the moon than they could on Earth. They could jump eight feet in one step!

The astronauts weighed less on the moon, but not because they were smaller. They were the same size and shape as they had been on Earth. They just weighed less.

The astronauts said walking on the moon felt like floating.

How much would you weigh on the moon? You can **divide** to find out. The boy in these pictures weighs 60 pounds on Earth. To find out how much he would weigh on the moon, divide 60 by 6. The number you get is how much the boy would weigh if he were on the moon.

60 pounds on Earth

60 ÷ 6 = 10

A boy who weighs 60 pounds on Earth would weigh 10 pounds on the moon.

**10 pounds
on the moon**

How heavy was Neil Armstrong on the moon? On Earth he weighed about 360 pounds with his space suit on. You can divide to find out how much he weighed on the moon.

Use a **calculator**.

- Press 3 and 6 and 0 for Neil Armstrong's weight.
- Press the divide key (÷).
- Press 6.
- Press the equal key (=) to find the answer.

Neil Armstrong weighed 60 pounds on the moon.

Neil Armstrong's space suit was heavier on Earth than it was on the moon.

calculator   a machine that helps people do math

divide   to separate into equal groups

gravity   a force that pulls objects toward Earth

mission   a task

weight   the amount of heaviness

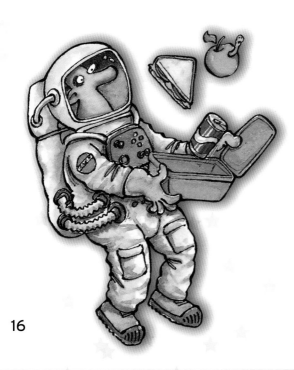